THE IDEAL

POLITICIAN

- ❖ PREFACE
- ❖ THE CURRENT BREED
- ❖ DESIRED PERSONALITY TRAITS
- ❖ IMPACT OF VOTERS' IDEOLOGY
- ❖ IMAGE OF THE IDEAL POLITICIAN
- ❖ THE SEARCH PROCESS
- ❖ INDIAN CONTEXT
- ❖ INTERNATIONAL ARENA
- ❖ ROLE OF ELECTIONS
- ❖ OUR BULLET POINTS

PREFACE

Many at times, we are faced with a dilemma as to what we should do in order to make our country a developed one. We tend to pass the buck on to others but seldom do we realize that it is we, i.e., the children of Mother India who should take individualistic responsibility to usher in a growth in our beloved nation. And the first step towards this goal is to choose a person who is an expert in development agenda as our leader. If we choose a leader who is well-versed in his efforts and knowledge to develop the nation, then half of the job is done. One has to keep in mind that our chosen person has to be a leader in the true sense and not merely a politician. Or rather a leader should be the ideal politician.

THE CURRENT BREED

It can be rightly said that India and the world have developed a lot over the years but what remains lacking is the sheer apathy of rulers and politicians of developing and undeveloped nations towards the common man. India, somehow doesn't fall in this league. Our leaders, belonging to every party, whether Congress, BJP or Janata tried and are still trying their level best to put the nation on the path of rapid development. Keeping in view of the current political situation in India, the current breed should really pull up their socks to push India towards massive developmental and industrialization process like those which have happened in the East Asian, Japanese, Chinese and Korean Economies.

DESIRED PRSONALITY TRAITS

An Ideal Politician in our view should exhibit desired personality traits. This would hold true for the entire breed encompassing all nations.

He should be more stable. He should be an extrovert. He should be wishing to do one's work or duty well and more thoroughly. He should be more open and honest than the voter himself. Other major virtues could be a sense of discipline, immense trustworthiness, courage, humaneness and intelligence. He should be unassuming, forgiving and a person who is able to build up consensus in order to bring people across party lines on the same page in order to pass major laws for development of the nation.

IMPACT OF VOTERS' IDEOLOGY

There is no doubt that personality of a politician is of supreme importance. Voters are very clear about the fact that their chosen politicians should have personality similar to what they visualise about.

And it is also true that politicians try to match up to the expectations in terms of personality of their voters. The role of personality in politics has been a domain of interest to politicians and social scientists for many years. Recent research primarily focused on how actual politicians are perceived and how voters' and politicians' personalities match. However, little attention has been paid to the direct assessment of what exactly voters believe to be the *ideal* personality profile of politicians. If we take into consideration the present times, politicians are rather very careful about how they would be able to match the ideology of the voters. Voters want their politicians to be more receptive. They prefer their leaders to visit their constituencies more often so that they can put up their grievances to them and their issues get resolved in due course of time. It is a well-known fact that if the aspirations of the people are in tune with strategic goals of development of the politicians, then the growth of the nation as a whole is bound to happen.

IMAGE OF THE IDEAL POLITICIAN

Nowadays, a very important phenomenon is that politicians are very interested in building up an image for themselves which would help them to remain in power for long and above all establish a greater connect with the people so that they are in a better position to serve them.

Also, the people of their constituencies prefer that their leaders have a pro poor and pro-development image.

To develop such an image, politicians use the services of PR firms, individuals and even the bureaucrats who serve under them. It is a well-known fact that a very famous and renowned bureaucrat in Gujarat helped build our current Prime Minister's image amongst the common man, the industry and the overall political galaxy.

Once the image is built up, it is again the duty of the politician to carry it for long or rather improvise upon it further if he/she has to continue winning elections and remain in power for long enough.

Also, image building is to be done very meticulously and carefully so that it doesn't get interpreted in a wrong sense and also it doesn't become the target for being misused by opposition leaders.

THE SEARCH PROCESS

Sometimes it is very hard to choose the correct leader. There are too many political parties. This tends to a lot of confusion. It is important to decipher what is good for us, our family and our community, and to stand up for what we believe in. That's why it's very important to vote for our kind of leader. We should vote for policies and not personalities. We should first know our candidates thoroughly. We should then perform lot of research on them. We shouldn't vote for someone just because they are a part of certain party. We shouldn't vote based upon what others are doing. We should base our voting process off our research. We should also ensure that the candidate we are voting for has addressed every issue. And then we should proceed to vote when we have successfully accomplished all the above tasks.

INDIAN CONTEXT

A good politician should not crave for money and power. They should be sharp and not cheat the public. They should come out of their stereotyped image and think about the development of the country.

India is witnessing a drastic change in politics. Newer political parties are desperate to seek power and old, experienced ones are lethargic enough to act fast on the development plank. Indian politicians also have a habit of blame game. What one party does, is condemned by the other party. Regular clashes and critical remarks on one another are all common to watch on television. But amid all this hullaballoo, India needs good politicians. Some even argue that the youth can bring the desired change in our society. Leading political parties are now taking the youth along with them. Now, who knows if their interest is in the development of youth or vote bank as every third person in India is youth. Youth can certainly bring change because of fresh ideas but with them comes the energy, and if this energy is uncontrolled, it can do more harm than good. To balance that energy, there must be some experienced politicians in the squad.

It is worthy to be noted that every government in India has a record of doing something good for our poor brethren. The Congress government was pro poor and the BJP government did a lot in improving Indian infrastructure, particularly roads.

INTERNATIONAL ARENA

Looking beyond India, we can summarize that politician have been particularly instrumental in improving the lives of people and economies of the countries' which they have ruled. Glaring examples have been Japan, South Korea and the Asian Tigers.

However, on the contrary, certain nations' leaders have pushed their countries' economies towards deceleration. Examples being Iran, Afghanistan, Zimbabwe, Sri Lanka amongst others.

On one hand there have been statesmen like Shinzo Abe, Lee Kuan Yew and on the other hand there have been looters like Gotabaya Rajpaksha and Robert Mugabe.

So, there is a variety of leaders to look up to around the world.

As regards to the USA and Europe, their leaders have been charismatic and enigmatic in maintain their growth records. However, in these nations, the institutions have been quite strong in maintaining the growth trajectory of these nations like we have seen recently the example of Great Britain.

ROLE OF ELECTIONS

Elections contribute greatly to democratic governance. Because direct democracy—a form of government in which political decisions are made directly by the entire body of qualified citizens—is impractical in most modern societies, democratic government must be conducted through representatives. Elections enable voters to select leaders and to hold them accountable for their performance in office. Accountability can be undermined when elected leaders do not care whether they are reelected or when, for historical or other reasons, one party or coalition is so dominant that there is effectively no choice for voters among alternative candidates, parties, or policies. Nevertheless, the possibility of controlling leaders by requiring them to submit to regular and periodic elections helps to solve the problem of succession in leadership and thus contributes to the continuation of democracy. Moreover, where the electoral process is competitive and forces candidates or parties to expose their records and future intentions to popular scrutiny, elections serve as forums for the discussion of public issues and facilitate the expression of public opinion.

Elections thus provide political education for citizens and ensure the responsiveness of democratic governments to the will of the people. They also serve to legitimize the acts of those who wield power, a function that is performed to some extent even by elections that are noncompetitive.

Elections also reinforce the stability and legitimacy of the political community. Like national holidays commemorating common experiences, elections link citizens to each other and thereby confirm the viability of the polity. As a result, elections help to facilitate social and political integration.

Finally, elections serve a self-actualizing purpose by confirming the worth and dignity of individual citizens as human beings. Whatever other needs voters may have, participation in an election serves to reinforce their self-esteem and self-respect. Voting gives people an opportunity to have their say and, through expressing partisanship, to satisfy their need to feel a sense of belonging. Even nonvoting satisfies the need of some people to express their alienation from the political community. For precisely these reasons, the long battle for the right to vote and the demand for equality in electoral participation can be viewed as the manifestation of a profound human craving for personal fulfillment.

OUR BULLET POINTS

Every ruling party in its present time always tries to keep on building their images via print media or other media or by the implementation of their policies in Government, Semi-Government or Private organizations. Although, there is nothing wrong in this process, but unfortunately, it is quite but natural that when someone, be it a political party, a politician or their ideology tries to convey to the masses about the sorry state of affairs of the incumbent political party, then in this process, the whole sort of positive perks which was being enjoyed by the masses of the country also gets wiped away. And whereas, with the passage of time, the parties of the present times try to keep on rebuilding their images, the general masses on the contrary get lost and confused in this turbulent turmoil.